George Washington Carver

JUNIOR ■ WORLD ■ BIOGRAPHIES
A JUNIOR *BLACK AMERICANS OF ACHIEVEMENT* BOOK

George Washington Carver

LOIS P. NICHOLSON

CHELSEA JUNIORS
a division of CHELSEA HOUSE PUBLISHERS

FRONTISPIECE: *Born a slave, George Washington Carver lived to become a noted botanist, inventor, and ecologist; a champion of southern poverty-stricken black farmers; and a beloved national public figure.*

English-language words that are italicized in the text can be found in the glossary at the back of the book.

Chelsea House Publishers

EDITORIAL DIRECTOR   Richard Rennert
EXECUTIVE MANAGING EDITOR   Karyn Gullen Browne
COPY CHIEF   Robin James
PICTURE EDITOR   Adrian G. Allen
ART DIRECTOR   Robert Mitchell
MANUFACTURING DIRECTOR   Gerald Levine

JUNIOR WORLD BIOGRAPHIES

SENIOR EDITOR   Ann-Jeanette Campbell
SERIES DESIGN   Marjorie Zaum

Staff for GEORGE WASHINGTON CARVER
EDITORIAL ASSISTANT   Kelsey Goss
PICTURE RESEARCHER   Sandy Jones
COVER ILLUSTRATION   Richard Daskam

Copyright © 1994 by Chelsea House Publishers, a division of Main Line Book Co. All rights reserved. Printed and bound in the United States of America.

3 5 7 9 8 6 4

Library of Congress Cataloging-in-Publication Data
Nicholson, Lois, 1949–
   George Washington Carver / Lois P. Nicholson.
   p. cm.—(Junior world biographies)
   Includes bibliographical references (p.) and index.
ISBN 0-7910-1763-X.
      0-7910-2114-9 (pbk.)
   1. Carver, George Washington, 1864?–1943—Juvenile literature. 2. Afro-American agriculturalists—Biography—Juvenile literature. 3. Agriculturalists—United States—Biography—Juvenile literature. [1. Carver, George Washington, 1864?–1943. 2. Agriculturalists. 3. Afro-Americans—Biography.] I. Title. II. Series.
S417.C3N53 1994
630'.92—dc20   93-38515
                                                                                              CIP

Contents

1	Kidnapped	7
2	The Quest To Learn	17
3	The Tuskegee Professor	29
4	The Creative Scientist	43
5	A Folk Hero's Fame	53
6	To Be Remembered	63
	Further Reading	72
	Glossary	73
	Chronology	75
	Index	78

*In 1855, Moses Carver purchased Mary,
the 13-year-old slave who would become
George Washington Carver's mother.
This is his receipt.*

> Received of Moses Carver Seven Hundred Dollars in full consideration for a Negro girl named Mary, age about thirteen years who I warrant to be sound in body and mind and a slave for life
> Given under my hand and seal this 9th day of October A.D. 1855—
> Witness
> Jno. Dade Jr.
> +Wm P. McGinnis (Seal)

CHAPTER

1
Kidnapped

One cold winter night toward the end of the Civil War, on a farm near Diamond, Missouri, an infant slave slept in a simple cabin with his brother and mother. Their owner slept nearby in a house scarcely larger than the slaves' cabin. Suddenly, the peaceful night was shattered by the thundering approach of galloping horses.

Moses Carver, the slaves' owner, awoke with a start, fearful that the men on horseback were *night raiders*. Throughout the Civil War, renegades from the Union Army, bushwhackers from the Confederate Army, and civilian outlaws alike raided farms for goods and money. Confederate raiders were also known to kidnap slaves and sell them to new owners. During the last few years, Moses Carver's farm had been raided three times, and once he was tortured to reveal where he had hidden his money.

    The infant slave's mother, Mary, tried desperately to escape with her two sons, but before she could get out of the cabin, the kidnappers grabbed her, with the baby in her arms. Carver rushed to the scene too late to save Mary and her infant, but in time to rescue the older boy, Jim. As quickly as they had come, the kidnappers disappeared with their loot. Carver vowed to find Mary and the baby, George, and bring them back home.

    Moses Carver and his wife, Susan, believed it was wrong to own slaves, but their 240-acre farm was prosperous and they needed help to keep it going. Because land was cheap and plentiful, many laborers bought their own farms instead of working for someone else. The Carvers had raised Moses's orphaned nieces and nephews who were of great help with the work, but the children were grown and living on their own. So, in 1855, Moses Carver bought the then 13-year-old Mary from a neighbor.

It is unclear who fathered Mary's sons and whether she may also have had twin daughters, or more children, who had died in infancy. In 1860, she gave birth to Jim. Later, around 1864, she had a second son who was named George Washington. As was common practice with slaves, Jim and George took their owner's last name of Carver.

The Carvers had always been kind to Mary and her sons (with the major exception that they had not given the slaves their freedom), and now they hired a neighbor, former Union scout John Bentley, to search for Mary and George. Several days after the kidnapping, Bentley rode into Diamond on horseback, with George Washington Carver in his arms. Bentley had located the baby in Arkansas, but either George's mother had died, or he was unable to find any trace of her. Moses Carver rewarded Bentley with a prized possession: one of the racehorses he had raised on his farm.

On December 18, 1865, the 13th Amendment to the Constitution went into effect, granting freedom to all slaves in the United States. Moses and Susan Carver changed from being Jim and George's owners to being their foster parents.

It was unusual for white parents to raise black children, but the Carvers had a reputation for being unconventional, even eccentric. Although they kept to themselves, they were respected by their neighbors because of their prosperity. Moses was known to be a fine fiddler and very good with animals, including the racehorses he trained. While George remembered Moses and Susan as loving parents, he also said, "There are so many things that naturally I erased from my mind. There are so many things that an orphan child does not want to remember."

Even as a child, George had a reputation for his botanical skills. In and around Diamond, Missouri, he was known as the "plant doctor."

Jim, who was five years older than George, and the stronger of the two boys, helped Moses with the strenuous work in the fields. George, a frail and sickly child, helped Susan around the house with such tasks as cooking meals, mending clothing, and tending the garden.

George quickly demonstrated a special interest in the plants under his care, experimenting with various soils and growing conditions. The local people called him the "plant doctor" and asked his advice on raising their own plants and flowers. The Carvers recognized the boy's rare gift and encouraged his talents.

George's general curiosity and appreciation of nature was obvious from a young age. He eagerly explored the nearby woods and fields, collecting *specimens* of many plants and creatures. In fact, after running across one too many of George's live specimens indoors, Susan Carver from then on made him empty his pockets before entering the house. "I wanted to know every strange stone, flower, insect, bird, or beast,"

Carver later recalled. The only reference book in the house, *Webster's Elementary Spelling Book*, did not answer George's advanced questions.

It is not known how much religion was stressed in the Carver household, but George grew up to be a very religious man. He and his brother, Jim, attended church on Sundays, and by the time he was 10, George was a Christian. His view of God was first and foremost as God the Creator, and he connected his religious beliefs to his observations of all the living things in nature. Throughout his life, George kept his strong religious faith, and people were inspired by his views on nature and religion.

Before the Civil War, laws prohibited teaching slaves to read and write. When the war ended in 1865, however, schools were supposedly open to black children. Jim and George enrolled in a local school that met in the church where they worshiped, but they were turned away because they were black. The Carvers supported George's quest for an education and in 1876 provided him

Before the Civil War, it was commonly illegal to teach slaves to read. The classrooms where Carver was a young student were probably a lot more rustic than this one photographed in 1910.

with a tutor. Unfortunately, the tutor did not have enough knowledge to answer George's questions. Soon, George began to look elsewhere for his education. This was the beginning of the very long and hard search that would dominate George's entire childhood and youth.

At age 13, George walked the eight miles from Diamond to Neosho, Missouri, where he could attend a school for blacks. There he stayed with Andrew and Mariah Watkins, a childless black couple. He earned his keep by working around the house before and after school—and even during recess, when he would help Mariah with the laundry. George soon found, however, that the small school in Neosho lacked the educational challenge he wanted. His desire to know always outdid his instructors' abilities to teach.

Determined to expand his knowledge, George was forced to travel even greater distances from the Carver farm in Diamond, Missouri. In 1878, Moses and Susan Carver received the news that George had moved to Fort Scott, Kansas.

Carver was the only black student at Simpson College in 1890, but he did not feel that his skin color made a difference in how he was treated there.

CHAPTER

2

The Quest To Learn

Fort Scott, Kansas, promised a new life for George. He found employment, using the domestic skills he had learned from Susan Carver and Mariah Atkins, and he enrolled in school to further his education. On the evening of March 29, 1879, however, whatever hopes George had for his future in Fort Scott came to a violent end.

A black man had been imprisoned in Fort Scott, accused of raping a 12-year-old white girl.

After sundown, about 1,000 citizens gathered to watch as a mob of white men raided the jail and hauled the prisoner outside. A rope was tied around his neck, and the mob dragged him through the streets before hanging him from a lamppost and setting fire to his body.

While George had not encountered violence of this sort before, it was not so rare in Kansas, or elsewhere in the United States, at this time. Fearing for his own safety and well-being, he quickly fled Fort Scott. George could not, however, escape what he had seen that night; it was etched forever in his memory. When Carver was an old man, he said, "As young as I was, the horror haunted me and does even now."

George resumed his education in Olathe, Kansas, supporting himself by keeping house for a black couple, Ben and Lucy Seymour. In 1879, when the Seymours moved to Minneapolis, Kansas, George stayed behind, moving to nearby Paola where he worked as a family domestic while he finished the school term.

In 1880, George joined the Seymours in Minneapolis, where he entered a mostly white high school. George's earlier *botanical* interests were now joined by passions for music and painting. To support himself while studying, he opened a laundry in a shack located nearby in a ravine called Poverty Gulch.

In the summer of 1883, George journeyed by train to Missouri to visit his family. Moses, Susan, Jim, and George enjoyed a warm reunion and rejoiced in George's recent accomplishments. Upon returning to Kansas, George sadly learned that his brother Jim had meanwhile died of smallpox. The two boys had grown up sharing each other's sorrows, and George felt a great loss with his brother's death.

The following year, George finished high school and went to Kansas City, where he found employment as a typist. Before long, he sent an application to Highland College in Highland, Kansas, again in search of higher education. He was accepted, and in 1885 he arrived at the college to register for classes. When the college officials saw that George was black, however, they refused to admit him. Disheartened by this shocking and humiliating experience, George abandoned his plans for further schooling.

In Highland, George worked for a white family by the name of Beeler, again cleaning, cooking, and laundering. Members of the Beeler family had recently founded a town called Beeler, Kansas, a new settlement for *homesteaders* near the Colorado border. In 1886, George decided to create a new life for himself there.

Under the Homestead Act of 1862, anyone could have 160 acres of public land by filing a claim and paying a small registration fee. George obtained land south of Beeler in Ness County, Kansas, where he built a house of *sod* bricks, as did all the homesteaders. George found acceptance among the white settlers and quickly became an important part of the growing community.

George's modest home was similar to those of the others, but differed in one significant way.

In 1886, Carver built a sod house similar to this one on land he bought near the Kansas-Colorado border. Three years later he left it to continue his education.

It featured a *conservatory* filled with native plants, which George faithfully nurtured. He also furthered his scientific interests by collecting local mineral and rock samples.

George was continually frustrated by the effects of the harsh climate upon his crops. The 17 acres of corn and other vegetables he planted suffered from a lack of water. The winters were brutal: while George survived the severe blizzard of 1888, the storm killed more than 200 people.

The hard life of a homesteader was not right for George. He left Ness County in 1889, but felt that his time there had been worthwhile: "I want to say . . . to the good people of Ness County, that I owe much to them for what little I have been able to accomplish, as I do not recall a single instance in which I was not given an opportunity to develop the best that was within me."

With customary vigor, George relocated to Winterset, Iowa, where he worked in a hotel and set up a laundry to support himself. At the church he attended there, he met Dr. and Mrs. John Milholland, a wealthy white couple who were struck by George's already vast knowledge. They strongly urged the 25-year-old man to resume his quest for education.

In September 1890, George entered Simpson College in Indianola, Iowa. The officials at Simpson were impressed by George's thirst for knowledge, and they did not care about the color of his skin. George was the only black student on the campus, but it did not seem to matter to anyone. He expressed his contentedness in a letter to the Milhollands: "The people are very kind to me here and the students are wonderfully good. . . . I have the name unjustly of having one of the broadest minds in the school."

George turned his attention to painting while at Simpson. Flowers were frequently the subject of George's paintings, and he continued to nurture his own collection of plants, but painting—not botany—was, at this time, his primary interest. He thought of becoming an artist.

Etta Budd, George's painting teacher in the all-female art department, was herself the daughter of a *horticulture* professor. She discouraged his artistic pursuits, fearing he could not earn a living as a painter, but urged him to enroll in her father's school, the Iowa State College of Agriculture and Mechanical Arts, in Ames. In thinking over his options, George began to feel that God had called him for a career in science rather than art, though painting would remain a lifelong activity. About this, he would later write, "I realize that God has great work for me to do."

At first, George was unhappy at Iowa State. Following his arrival in August of 1891, he wrote,

Carver's first passion in college was painting, and he hoped to become an artist. His teacher suggested he pursue horticulture, the science of growing plants.

"The helpful means for a Christian growth is not so good." Not only was he homesick, but he met racial *prejudice* in Ames. He was not allowed to live in the school dormitory with the other students, and he was even required to eat his meals in the basement with the kitchen employees. Over the next five years, George overcame his unhappiness as he began to make friends and participate in various campus activities. He joined school organizations—from the debating club to the German club—founded the Agricultural Society, and became the Iowa State football team's first trainer and *masseur*.

Alongside his extracurricular activities, George spent the time and energy required on his studies to earn high grades and praise from his professors. His skills at grafting plants (growing a part of one plant onto another), cross-fertilizing (combining cells from two different plants), and creating hybrids (cross-fertilizing different plants to form new ones) were universally admired.

According to one professor, "Carver is by all means the ablest student we have."

George dedicated himself to scientific study at Ames, but painting remained a great love. Encouraged to enter his paintings in a state art exhibition in 1892, George hesitated because he had neither the money to make the trip nor a good suit to wear. His friends, however, provided him with both a train ticket and a new suit. Not only did one of his paintings win a prize, but George was selected to represent Iowa at the 1893 World's Columbian Exposition in Chicago, one of the greatest world fairs in history.

In 1894, George proudly received his bachelor of agriculture degree. He stayed at Ames, teaching freshman courses while furthering his own studies. Several black colleges learned of George's excellent reputation and sought to recruit him, but George was determined to earn his graduate degree. Then, in March 1896, a letter arrived from a man who was emerging as a black leader in the nation. His name was Booker T.

Washington, principal of the Tuskegee Normal and Industrial Institute, and George could not ignore his invitation to join the faculty there.

Located in Alabama, Tuskegee Institute was founded in 1881 as a *vocational training* school for black students. At the time that Booker T. Washington wrote Carver, he was searching for a qualified candidate to head the school's new agricultural department. He knew Carver was the only black man in the country to have received a higher education in scientific agriculture, and he had decided that Carver was right for the job.

In response to Washington's invitation, Carver wrote, "It has always been the one ideal of my life to be of the greatest good to the greatest number of 'my people' possible and to this end I have been preparing myself for many years." Based on what he knew of Tuskegee Institute, he believed that an education received there was "the key to unlock the golden door of freedom to our people." He accepted Washington's offer.

Tuskegee Institute faculty (Carver, top row, fourth from left; Washington, front row, fourth from right) taught courses such as bricklaying, printing, and shoemaking, along with history, chemistry, and grammar.

CHAPTER

3

The Tuskegee Professor

Thirty-one-year-old George Washington Carver had spent most of his life among white people in the Midwest. When, in 1896, he arrived at Tuskegee Institute, an all-black school deep in the South, he found himself in a strange environment. The U.S. Supreme Court had recently passed the *Plessy v. Ferguson* decision, which permitted "separate but equal" facilities for blacks and whites. Blacks could legally be denied entrance into schools, movie theaters, or hotels based on the notion that such public places were for whites only. Blacks were also denied jobs, education, housing, and even the right to vote.

Tuskegee Institute provided an island of refuge from such a harsh reality. Booker T. Washington, Tuskegee Institute's first principal, was guiding the school on its way to becoming a first-class vocational training institution. Washington believed that blacks would gain social and political equality only after they had mastered the skills that would lead them to economic independence. He quickly became a leading spokesperson for many African Americans.

Booker T. Washington, the founder and first principal of Tuskegee Institute, was also an early spokesperson for African Americans.

Carver, who shared Washington's theory and vision, plunged into his heavy work load, which included creating the new agricultural department, teaching classes, conducting indoor and outdoor research, overseeing the maintenance of the school's grounds, and, temporarily, serving as the school's veterinarian. He seemed born to be a teacher, inspiring students with his love of nature and his fascination with botany, *chemistry,* and agriculture.

Professor Carver did not merely lecture his students; he encouraged them to learn by experience. He took them on field trips where they collected plant and mineral specimens. An ecologist before his time, he taught that everything in nature was interrelated, and that a balance between nature's elements must be kept. Carver was popular among the students, who appreciated his immense store of knowledge. As a practical joke, one day some of his students constructed a fake insect from the parts of different insects for Carver

In his laboratory at Tuskegee Institute, Carver (second from right) taught his students through agricultural research and experiments.

to identify. The professor was not fooled. He identified the strange specimen as a *humbug.*

Tuskegee Institute's agricultural experiment station—10 acres of land where research was conducted—thrived under Carver's direction. He concentrated on the search for farming methods that would benefit poor farmers (sometimes called dirt farmers) and sharecroppers (or tenant farmers). Sharecroppers were farmers who tilled someone else's land for a small share of the profits, and many poor black and white families were trapped in the sharecropping system. They usually spent their entire lives farming wealthy landowners' property without ever being able to save enough money to buy their own land. In order for the farmer to ever benefit under this system, the land would have to produce more.

Carver knew that the soil in the South was virtually worn out from repeated plantings of cotton, the most popular Southern crop. "The average farmer," he said, "goes on trying to raise cotton in the same old way, which means nothing but failure, more or less, for him."

To solve this problem, Carver championed crop rotation—planting different crops in the same soil on a rotating basis. The crops were selected so that each would enrich the soil that had been exhausted by the previous crop, preparing it for the following crop. Additionally, Carver taught the importance of using *organic fertilizer* to replace the soil's lost nutrients. Finally, he introduced new crops that farmers could sell on the market as well as serve at their own kitchen tables (sharecroppers generally could not afford to buy their food from a store).

With these ideas in mind, Tuskegee Institute's scientist experimented with crops such as peanuts, sweet potatoes, black-eyed peas, alfalfa, velvet beans, and soybeans. Just experimenting and lecturing, however, were not enough for Carver. He wanted not only to teach his students at the institute but to better the lives of the dirt farmers and sharecroppers. He used his experience as a teacher to figure out the best way to teach these other "students," the rural poor.

Until this time, scientific information had been written in such a way that the average person could not understand it. Carver realized that "the man farthest down," the sharecropper and dirt farmer, must be able to understand the information about new crops in order to follow the instructions for them. This simple but important realization set Carver's work apart from that of his colleagues.

Carver used the findings of the agricultural experiment station at Tuskegee Institute (below) to help the dirt farmers and sharecroppers in the South (above) make a better living for themselves.

In 1898, Carver began producing newsletters for sharecroppers and their families. These bulletins were easy to read and provided recipes as well as information about farming. The same publication that introduced new crops would give directions on how to prepare and preserve them for the family's use. *How To Grow the Peanut and 105 Ways of Preparing it for Human Consumption* and *When, What, and How To Can and Preserve Fruits and Vegetables in the Home* proved highly successful. Regardless of how useful the bulletins were, however, Carver did not believe that they were enough.

Before Carver's arrival at Tuskegee Institute, Booker T. Washington had made frequent visits to tenant farmers and had been shocked by the level of their poverty. They existed on a diet of pork fat and corn bread, and entire families lived in one-room cabins. Just talking with the farmers about their living conditions—and, later, publishing bulletins—fell far short of what was needed. Washington decided to create an outreach program. When Carver came to Tuskegee Institute, he embraced the principal's goal to reach beyond the walls of the school to the people.

In 1892, Washington had held the first farmers' conference at Tuskegee Institute. He invited 75 farmers and people from other walks of life, but approximately 400 people showed up. The program's success prompted him to hold the conference annually.

Carver realized that such programs were only meeting the needs of the better-informed farmers. Many poor farmers would have no way of knowing about the conferences, let alone of coming to Tuskegee to participate. So Carver decided to make his knowledge—as a teacher, agriculturist, and ecologist—available to as many people as possible by traveling to them.

As Booker T. Washington had done before him, Carver visited the homes of the rural poor and talked with them about their farming methods. Not only was he able to pass on his information, but the visits gave him firsthand knowledge of the farmers' problems, which told him where he needed to focus his work.

Carver also started monthly meetings of what he called the Farmers' Institute. There he would talk about crop rotation, fertilizers, and soil depletion. Farmers would bring in samples of their crops for Carver to analyze. As the meetings grew more popular, kitchen demonstrations were set up to show how to preserve and prepare specific foods. During the winter months, when farmers had less work to do, Tuskegee Institute offered a two-week course covering a wide variety of practical farming knowledge and advice. In eight years, the number of students attending this winter course rose from 20 to 1,500. Carver's extension programs became models in black schools throughout the region, and he was often invited to speak at conferences.

At the beginning of the 20th century, the South had very strict racial laws and customs, which discouraged social contact between whites and blacks. In 1902, Carver went to Ramer,

Alabama, to attend a farmers' conference at a black college. He was accompanied by a white female photographer named Frances B. Johnston. Nelson E. Henry, a black teacher from the school, met the pair at the train station after dark.

The sight of a white woman with two black men at first dismayed and then angered some of Ramer's white citizens. In a letter describing the incident to Booker T. Washington, Carver wrote that a crowd had gathered at the station just "to see what would happen."

The threesome left the station in a buggy, to take the photographer to the home of a black family where she was going to spend the night. On the way, however, they decided that it would be safer for her to stay in town. They dropped Carver off at his lodging and then returned to Ramer.

Carver's letter to Washington reported that on the way back Henry "was met by parties and after a few words was shot at three times." Henry fled as the photographer Johnston ran back to the house where Carver was staying. "I got out at once," wrote Carver, "and succeeded in getting her to the next station where she took the train the next morning. . . . I had to walk nearly all night . . . to stay out of [the whites'] reach." Returning to Ramer in daylight, he found that "everything was in a state of turbulency and a mob had been formed to locate Mr. Henry and deal with him."

Following Carver's return to Tuskegee, the institute investigated the incident. Despite the efforts of some of the citizens of Ramer to play down the episode, Henry resigned his teaching position, and the school moved farther out of town. In recalling the event, Carver claimed that it was "the most frightening experience of my life."

Carver designed the Jesup Wagon to take agricultural exhibits and demonstrations to the people where they lived.

Carver did not allow the incident at Ramer, or the possibility of others like it, to keep him from continuing his outreach programs. Acting on another of Booker T. Washington's ideas, Carver designed and outfitted a wagon with materials for agricultural demonstrations and exhibitions. He called this wagon a movable school. Built by Tuskegee Institute students, it was partially funded by Morris K. Jesup, a New York banker, and was called the Jesup Wagon. Soon, the U.S. Department of Agriculture (USDA) became aware of the project and wanted to play a part in its mission. In 1906, the USDA took over the Jesup Wagon, assigning its supervision to a former student of Carver's, Thomas Campbell, who became the USDA's first black demonstration agent.

Carver was never content to wait for students to come and find him at Tuskegee Institute. Instead, he took his knowledge out into the world for any and all who would listen. This set him far apart from other scientists.

Carver was as comfortable at his speaking engagements as he was in his laboratory, always furthering the cause of poor farmers in the United States.

CHAPTER

4

The Creative Scientist

In addition to his outdoor experiments and extension programs, Carver conducted research in an indoor laboratory at Tuskegee Institute. When the young scientist arrived in 1896, there had been no laboratory so he had to create his own, rummaging through junk piles and garbage for bottles and jars to use as equipment. It was not until 14 years later—in 1910—that Carver was even promised a fully equipped laboratory. More years had to pass before it became a reality. Throughout, Carver used this makeshift laboratory in his pursuit of ways to better the crops, diets, and economic standing of sharecroppers.

One of the ways Carver conducted his laboratory research was by analyzing soil samples. He would study the dirt in order to determine what fertilizers would replenish its nutrients after growing crops had exhausted it. He also studied the dietary value of different crops, which led him to develop recipes using peanuts, sweet potatoes, and black-eyed peas.

Carver dreamed of economic success for the tenant farmers in the South and worked tirelessly toward it. He searched for chemical methods that would ensure that success, calling this "creative chemistry." For instance, in 1911, Carver tried to produce paints and wood stains from Alabama's clay soil, but he was not successful. He developed a method of preserving pork, but no meat company could be convinced to try it. Although disappointed when his projects failed, Carver continued to dream of creating many products that would bring wealth to poor southern farmers.

Carver worked hard to make sure that the news of his agricultural experiments spread beyond the walls of Tuskegee Institute. Because he was a popular and eager speaker, he was invited to give talks at many engagements. Increasingly, people began to learn of his accomplishments and, before long, his name was famous throughout the South.

Then, in 1915, Carver's friend and colleague Booker T. Washington suddenly died. Saddened by Washington's death, Carver became depressed and stopped teaching for a time. The two men had frequently disagreed about matters at Tuskegee Institute, which Carver felt had perhaps hidden their close bond. He wrote, "I am sure Mr. Washington never knew how much I loved him and the cause for which he gave his life."

Robert Russa Morton, Tuskegee Institute's new principal, released Carver from many of his duties in the classroom. Eventually, Carver taught only during summer sessions. The Tuskegee scientist now could devote much more time to research.

The new administration at Tuskegee Institute recognized Carver as someone who could bring good publicity to the school. He was featured in the school's publications, which increased his fame. In 1916, he was honored by England's Royal Society for the Encouragement of the Arts; he was the first black American to be recognized by this organization.

In 1917, the United States entered World War I. Suddenly, Carver's agricultural knowledge gained interest at the federal level. Food shortages developed as commercial trade throughout the world was disrupted by the war. The United States government sought the Tuskegee scientist's help in such areas as food preservation and substitution. In 1918, Carver traveled to Washington, D.C., primarily to share his bread-making techniques with the USDA. Carver's trick was to substitute

In his search for an economic breakthrough, Carver practiced "creative chemistry," which led him to discover new products and procedures related to agriculture.

flour made of sweet potatoes for some of the more commonly used wheat flour.

The great inventor Thomas Edison also sought Carver's services. He wished to hire the brilliant scientist away from Tuskegee Institute and was willing to pay a lot of money for him. The exact details about the job offer remain unclear, but Carver later reported that he turned it down because he did not wish to leave the South for Edison's laboratory in New Jersey. Carver seemingly could not turn his back on his lifelong goal to help rid the South of its economic problems.

While Carver's research interests were varied, it was the peanut that brought him his greatest fame. Much excitement followed his development of a process for making "peanut milk" in 1919, including coverage in the national magazine *Popular Mechanics*. It was later learned, however, that an Englishman had already patented the process in 1917. Disappointment at the news did not stop Carver or his supporters. The peanut producers valued and respected the work of this dedicated scientist and continued to sponsor his research.

The United Peanut Association of America invited Carver to address its 1920 convention in Montgomery, Alabama. Southern racial customs required that Carver, the guest speaker, take the freight elevator to the upstairs meeting room, instead of using the passenger elevator that was reserved for whites only.

Nonetheless, Carver impressed his all-white audience with his talk, "The Possibilities of the Peanut." In much the same fashion as he had entertained his students while lecturing, Carver captured the attention of his listeners by demonstrating the many uses of the peanut plant. Coverage of his presentation in the *Peanut Promoter* noted that he "verily won his way into the hearts of the peanut men."

In 1921, Carver appeared before Congress's House Ways and Means Committee in Washington, D.C., to advise on a peanut *tariff*. At first, the congressmen—all white men—were skeptical about about this 56-year-old black scientist who, as usual, was dressed in a rumpled suit with a flower in the lapel and who spoke in a high-pitched voice. But his combined wit and humor quickly *dispelled* the concerns of the politicians.

Like a magician pulling objects from a hat, Carver exhibited a variety of products made from peanuts during the 10 minutes that he was given to make his presentation: peanut milk, peanut candy, instant coffee, cosmetics, and breakfast foods. "Here is a breakfast food," he said, picking up one item. "I am very sorry that you cannot taste this, so I will taste it for you." The congressmen laughed as Carver ate the sample.

After he testified before a House committee in 1921 on various uses for the peanut, Carver—typically dressed in a rumpled suit, with a flower in his lapel—became a nationally recognized figure.

While most of the congressmen listened eagerly, one representative took the opportunity to make a racial joke. Unflappable as always, Carver answered the representative with a *retort* and continued his presentation. The committee was so obviously enjoying itself and learning something valuable that, when Carver's time was up, the chairman told him to keep on talking—his time was unlimited. The Tuskegee scientist continued to testify for nearly an hour.

The publicity that came from Carver's entertaining testimony before the House committee signaled the birth of his role as a national folk hero. Combining politeness, humor, and a mild manner, Carver was a genuine crowd-pleaser. He had the twin gifts of inspiring people to listen and giving them something to listen to. At nearly 60 years of age, George Washington Carver had a name that was known throughout the land. He had become a symbol of black achievement.

As a popular public figure, Carver used his fame to address his major concerns: nature, ecology, and the plight of the poor farmer.

CHAPTER

5
A Folk Hero's Fame

Following his appearance before the House Ways and Means Committee in Washington, D.C., Carver's fame grew. More than ever in the public eye, he spent the rest of his life balancing the variety of his interests with the demands of his popularity.

During the 1920s, almost all of Carver's research concentrated on his creative chemistry. Some companies, such as Ralston-Purina, expressed a serious interest in Carver's research and methods of production. But Carver maintained a busy schedule and did not have the time to pursue such commercial opportunities. To help out, he hired a young white man, Ernest Thompson, as his business manager.

Thompson's job was to look for investors and manufacturers who would be interested in Carver's projects. He planned an exhibit at the Cecil Hotel in Atlanta, Georgia, in 1923, which led to the formation of a company, known as the Carver Products Company. It was designed to sell Carver's formulas and processes for manufacturing. Four years later, however, the Carver Products Company had met with little success and quietly went out of existence.

Only one product of Carver's was manufactured and marketed during this period. Penol, a creamy mixture of creosote and peanuts, was made by the Carver Penol Company, which was founded in 1926. Creosote, a liquid distilled from wood tar, was used to treat tuberculosis and bronchitis. Carver added peanuts to give the medicine some nutritional value and prevent the nausea caused by swallowing the creosote alone.

Carver's mind was always active. But his tendency to jump from one project to another instead of following through caused many of his business problems. His commercial failures aside, the wide range of ideas with which he experimented was impressive: paper from peanut shells, man-made marble from wood shavings, cotton for paving roads, and artificial rubber made from sweet potatoes.

Carver's fame was unshaken by his lack of business success. Americans had discovered a new hero in the quiet agricultural scientist from Tuskegee Institute and he was unique. The public appreciated Carver's talent for explaining things in an understandable manner and valued his religious humility. When a reporter asked him about the lasting power of the paints he had made from clay, Carver replied, "Why should they not be permanent? God made the clay in the hills; they have been there for countless generations,

Carver's humble approach to nature was one of the many endearing qualities the public saw in him.

changeless. All I do is prepare what God has made. . . . It is God's work, not mine."

People also liked Carver's apparent simplicity. Money did not concern him. During his first 20 years at Tuskegee Institute, he did not receive a salary raise. Stories spread that he often left his paychecks in his desk, forgetting to cash them. He dressed in worn-out suits with his customary flower in the lapel.

Carver's popularity meant that he received honors from many different organizations. In one year, 1923, he was honored by both the conservative, white membership of the United Daughters of the Confederacy and the most prominent black power organization of the time, the National Association for the Advancement of Colored People (NAACP). The perspectives of these two organizations were sharply dissimilar, but each group saw in Carver a shining example of the successful black man in American society.

Carver chose not to speak out specifically about racial issues. The scientist limited his speeches to research topics, his views on nature, and his goal that the South would become an economically thriving region. Carver possessed, however, a rare gift for improving race relations by setting a personal example. One young man wrote to him, "You have shown me the one race, the human race. Color of skin or form of hair mean nothing to me now."

While Carver did not focus on racial issues, he was familiar with race-related incidents. Before he was to speak at a Young Men's Christian Association (YMCA) conference in Blue Ridge,

North Carolina, in 1924, Carver learned that a racial protest had been planned. A group of white participants intended to walk out during the lecture. While listening to Carver speak, however, the white delegates were so impressed by him that they never left the room. Following the lecture, one member of the group stood and apologized to the famous scientist.

The previous year at the YMCA conference in Blue Ridge, Carver had addressed another group of white attendees. In the audience, Carver spotted one particularly interested young man. After the speech, the young man, Jimmie Hardwick, told the scientist he would like to talk with him more. Carver replied, "Of course! I'd like you for one of my boys."

Carver's response puzzled Hardwick. A couple of days later the two men met. Carver explained that he had always been a bachelor and, since the death of his brother, he had no family—no blood relations—of his own. But he enjoyed taking a number of special students under his wing, and he considered them his adopted children. "In my work," explained Carver, "I meet young people who are seeking truth. God has given me some knowledge. When they will let me, I try to pass it on to my boys."

Through the years, there were many young people such as Jimmie Hardwick who became part

The death of his brother in 1883 left Carver without any biological relations; instead he formed close ties with many of his students, referring to them as his children.

of Carver's family. Everywhere Carver went, he met many individuals who were drawn to his kind and generous spirit. The letters they exchanged frequently expressed the caring that the students and their older friend and hero shared.

In 1924, Carver addressed a group of 500 people at the Marble Collegiate Church in New York City. There he spoke about the relationship between his religious beliefs and his scientific work. The audience warmly received his message, but two days later, the *New York Times* reacted differently to his speech. In an editorial, "Men of Science Never Talk That Way," the paper said that Carver lacked respect for scientific methods.

Hurt by the editorial, Carver responded in a letter saying, "Inspiration is never at variance with information." For Carver, religion and science were not at odds with each other. The *New York Times* never printed his letter, but other newspapers did. Many people agreed with Carver that no conflict existed between science and religion and were vocal in their support of the scientist. Just as he was deeply hurt by the editorial, so, too, was Carver moved by the many people who came to his defense during this episode.

In 1928, Carver received an honorary doctor of science degree from Simpson College. Although he would receive many honors, this one was especially pleasing because Simpson College was the first college he had attended. Also, for years many people had been mistakenly calling him "Dr. Carver"; now, he could claim that they were right.

In the 1920s, Carver was increasingly absent from his laboratory at Tuskegee Institute and more and more in the public's eye. Traveling and public speaking now allowed him to address a broader audience on his major themes: agricultural research, his views on nature and religion, and his dream for a healthy economy in the South. By tirelessly working toward his goals, he helped improve race relations along the way as he intended—by being an example of success.

Although an aging and famous scientist, Carver was still subjected to the common discrimination against African Americans.

CHAPTER

6

To Be Remembered

In 1932, an article entitled "A Boy Who Was Traded for a Horse" was published in *American Magazine*. It spread the image of Carver as the virtual inventor of the peanut, and as the humble, eccentric scientist who had begun his life as a slave. Although much had already been written about Carver, this article created great nationwide publicity and helped establish his place in American history. Five years later, the Tuskegee scientist was still so popular that the article was reprinted in *Reader's Digest.*

The Associated Press, a news agency whose articles are printed in newspapers across the country, published a profile on Carver in 1933. This story suggested that Carver had found a new therapy for victims of polio, a dreaded crippling disease. During the first half of the 20th century, the spread of polio reached epidemic proportions at times, but it was not until 1954 that a vaccine would become available. Patients began to flock to Tuskegee for Carver's treatment.

Carver treated his polio patients with a program that included massages with peanut oil. Following Carver's treatments, frail polio victims gained weight and showed improvement. When these patients reported how much better they felt, Carver became the object of even more publicity. He wrote, "Truly, God is speaking through the peanut oils I am working with. Marvelous, some come to me on crutches, canes, etc., and in time go away walking." Most of the medical experts, however, felt that the success of Carver's therapy was not due to the peanut oil he used, but to his massage technique.

During the Great Depression of the 1930s—a time when the country's economy collapsed and jobs, money, and food were scarce—Carver drew on his early experiences at Tuskegee Institute to teach families how to produce and preserve their own foods. He stressed the importance of diet, nutrition, and creative, healthful ways to feed a family on a limited budget. Carver found himself writing articles—on raising livestock, the use of natural fertilizers, and recipes for the foods produced, for example—similar to the pamphlets he had published at the turn of the century.

But Carver needed help to keep his busy schedule. In 1935, he hired a young man from Cornell University named Austin Curtis to be his assistant. Curtis, who sometimes referred to himself as "Baby Carver," became like a son to the elderly scientist whose health was failing. He not only helped Carver with his schedule but also assisted him with his research in the laboratory.

An important development took place in the United States in the 1930s, known as the chemurgic movement, or *chemurgy*. Its purpose was to create new agricultural products (such as juice concentrate) or more convenient ways of packaging old ones (such as freeze-dried vegetables). This was similar to what Carver had been researching all his life. In 1937, Carver addressed three different chemurgic conferences, but his greatest gain came from meeting the movement's best-known sponsor, Henry Ford. Ford, a pioneer in the field of automobile manufacturing, became Carver's best friend. Carver once wrote to him, "I consider you the greatest man I ever met."

By 1937, Carver also had participated on several national radio programs—the most up-to-date form of mass media and entertainment at the time. The Smithsonian Institution in Washington, D.C., produced a series of radio shows that told the story of the scientist's life. It aired throughout the country, spreading the fame of George Washington Carver.

The year 1937 also saw the celebration of Carver's 40th anniversary at Tuskegee Institute. A bronze bust of him was unveiled, speeches were made, and the event was widely publicized.

Hollywood, too, honored the scientist from Tuskegee. Metro-Goldwyn-Mayer (MGM) made a film called *The Story of Dr. Carver* in 1938. An actor played the role of the young George, but Carver played himself as the older scientist.

At the celebration in honor of Carver's 40 years at Tuskegee Institute, a bronze bust of the scientist was unveiled.

By this time, Carver had become a nationally recognized and honored figure, but because he was black, he continued to be the victim of racist practices. Just like every other African American, in the *segregated* South he could not use public facilities reserved for whites only. His friends would drive him to his engagements to spare him the humiliations of public transportation, which required all blacks to sit in the back of the vehicle.

In 1939, the 74-year-old Carver arrived at the New Yorker Hotel in New York City. He and Austin Curtis had reservations at the hotel, but they were told there were no rooms available and that they should leave. They refused to go. Suspicious that the hotel was discriminating against them because of their skin color, Curtis took action. He telephoned the publishing firm that was producing a book about Carver. The hotel management would not listen to the publisher's representative and still refused to give Carver and Curtis rooms.

Soon newspaper reporters began arriving, presumably called in by Carver's publisher. A white employee of the publishing company entered the hotel, asked for accommodations, and was given a room immediately. When he offered the room to Carver and Curtis, the hotel management again claimed there were no rooms available. The aging, famous scientist and his assistant waited for more than six hours in the hotel lobby until, finally, they were escorted to rooms. The incident received a lot of publicity as newspapers widely reported the event.

Carver's health began to decline in the 1930s. Because he wanted his life's work to be remembered and continued, he turned his energies to establishing a museum and laboratory in his name. Ironically, since as a student Carver had frequently supported himself by doing laundry, an old laundry building was converted into the George Washington Carver Museum and Foundation in Tuskegee. When the partially completed museum opened in 1939, some 2,000 people streamed into the monument to Carver's life.

Knowing that his life was coming to an end and wanting to leave a legacy, Carver cooperated with a writer on his biography. In 1940, Carver read the book's manuscript and was pleased. When the book still had not come out by 1942, he wrote to the publisher, "I was hoping so much that this book could be finished before it had to close with something sordid." Carver feared he would die before the book was published.

Late in 1942, Carver traveled to Dearborn, Michigan, to visit his friend, Henry Ford. Ford had just built a nutritional laboratory in Carver's honor and a replica of his childhood home. Speaking about his friend, Ford said, "In my opinion, Professor Carver has taken Thomas Edison's place as the world's greatest living scientist."

Carver (center) and Ford (right) stand in front of a replica of Carver's first home.

Upon Carver's return to Tuskegee in November, people noticed that he appeared frail. He continued his daily routines until one day in December when he fell while entering the Carver Museum. A few weeks later, on January 5, 1943, Carver died at the age of 77. He was buried on the campus of Tuskegee Institute, close to the grave of his friend Booker T. Washington.

George Washington Carver made many contributions to his country. He bettered himself through education and then, in turn, taught others. He promoted ecological as well as economic concerns when teaching about soil depletion, organic fertilizers, and crop rotation. He championed scientific reporting that was understandable to farmers as well as scientists. He provided a much-needed and respected role model for blacks when few existed. As a folk hero, he portrayed a successful postslavery black man. Perhaps his greatest and most lasting achievement was, as he wished, the personal example he set in his own kind, inquisitive, and generous life.

Further Reading

Elliot, Lawrence. *George Washington Carver: The Man Who Overcame.* Englewood Cliffs, NJ: Prentice-Hall, 1966.

Harlan, Louis R. *Booker T. Washington: The Wizard of Tuskegee, 1901–1915.* New York: Oxford University Press, 1983.

Kremer, Gary R. *George Washington Carver: In His Own Words.* Columbia: University of Missouri Press, 1986.

McMurry, Linda O. *George Washington Carver: Scientist and Symbol.* New York: Oxford University Press, 1981.

Manber, David. *Wizard of Tuskegee.* New York: Crowell-Collier, 1967.

Washington, Booker T. *Up from Slavery.* Garden City, NY: Doubleday, 1933.

Glossary

botanical having to do with the science of plants: their life, structure, growth, classification, etc.

chemistry the science dealing with the makeup and properties of substances

chemurgy the use of plants to produce new products: for example, using soybeans as a base for plastics

conservatory a room enclosed in glass for growing and displaying plants

dispel to drive or shoo away; to scatter

graft to insert a shoot or bud of one plant or tree into the stem or trunk of another

homesteader one who settled on a tract of land granted by the United States government

horticulture the science and art of growing fruits, vegetables, flowers, or ornamental plants

humbug something designed to deceive and mislead

masseur a man who practices massage and physical therapy

night raiders soldiers who performed acts of terror at night, such as kidnapping

organic fertilizer a natural substance, such as manure, used to restore richness and fertility to the land

prejudice a feeling or opinion, usually formed before all the facts are known

retort a quick, snappy answer often putting the recipient in his or her place

segregated restricted to members of one group or one race

sod a surface layer of earth containing grass plants and their matted roots

specimen a sample; one individual of a class or group

tariff a tax or duty that a government places on goods shipped into or out of the country

vocational training instruction in a skill or trade to be pursued as a career

Chronology

ca. 1864   Born George Washington Carver in Diamond, Missouri; is kidnapped and rescued

1865   Achieves freedom from slavery as the 13th Amendment to the U.S. Constitution is adopted

1877   Begins his formal education in Neosho, Missouri

1885   Carver's application to Highland College in Kansas is accepted, but his admission is denied on the basis of race

1886   Becomes a homesteader in Ness County, Kansas

1890   Enrolls at Simpson College in Iowa

1891   Transfers to Iowa State College of Agriculture and Mechanical Arts

1894   Receives a bachelor of agriculture degree; becomes a member of the Iowa State College faculty

1896 Receives a master of agriculture degree; becomes the director of agriculture and agricultural experiment station at Tuskegee Institute in Alabama

1898 Begins to publish agricultural bulletins for dirt farmers and their families as well as for scientists

1906 U.S. Department of Agriculture (USDA) adopts Carver's Jesup Wagon, designed for traveling agricultural exhibitions and demonstrations

1916 Carver is the first African American to be honored by England's Royal Society for the Encouragement of the Arts

1918 Engaged as a consultant in agricultural research by the USDA

1919 Develops peanut milk; discovers the formula is already patented

1921 Appears before a House Ways and Means Committee to advise on a peanut tariff

1923 Honored by both the United Daughters of the Confederacy and the National

Association for the Advancement of Colored People (NAACP)

1928 Receives honorary doctor of science degree from Simpson College

1933 Carver's peanut oil massages become widely publicized

1937 Meets and befriends Henry Ford, the automobile pioneer

1938 Appears in the film *The Story of Dr. Carver*

1943 Dies on January 5 in Tuskegee, Alabama

Index

"Boy Who Was Traded for a Horse, A" (article), 63

Carver, George Washington
attacked by *New York Times,* 60–61
childhood, 7–19
death, 71
as ecologist, 31, 37, 71
education, 13–20, 22–25
experiments with peanuts, 34, 36, 44, 48–50, 54, 55, 63, 64–65
fame, 48, 51, 53, 63, 64, 66, 67, 68, 69
as homesteader, 20–22
honors, 46, 56, 57, 61
interest in art, 19, 23, 25
inventions, 46–48, 50, 54, 55
laboratory research, 33, 43–46, 53–54, 61, 66
life as a slave, 7–10, 63
and polio therapy, 64–65
and racism, 7–10, 17–18, 24, 29, 38–40, 49, 57, 68–69
religious views, 13, 55, 56, 60, 61, 64
and the Tuskegee Institute, 27, 29–46, 61, 65, 67, 71
work with sharecroppers, 32–41, 61
writings, 36, 65
Carver, Jim (brother), 8, 9, 10, 12, 13, 19
Carver, Mary (mother), 8, 9, 10
Carver, Moses (owner, foster father), 7, 8, 9, 10, 12, 13, 15, 19
Carver, Susan (owner, foster mother), 8, 9, 10, 12, 13, 19
Carver Penol Company, 54
Chemurgy, 66

Department of Agriculture, U.S. (USDA), 41, 46
Diamond, Missouri, 7, 9, 15

Edison, Thomas, 48, 70

Farmers' conferences, 37, 39
Farmers' Institute, 38
Ford, Henry, 66, 70
Fort Scott, Kansas, 15, 17, 19

George Washington Carver Museum and Foundation, 69, 71

How To Grow the Peanut and 105 Ways of Preparing it for Human Consumption (newsletter), 36

Iowa State College of Agriculture and Mechanical Arts, 23, 24

Jesup Wagon, 40, 41

National Association for the Advancement of Colored People (NAACP), 57
Ness County, Kansas, 20, 21, 22

Peanut. *See* Carver, George Washington: experiments with peanuts

Penol, 54
Polio, 64
"Possibilities of the Peanut, The" (speech), 49

Ramer, Alabama, 39, 40
Royal Society for the Encouragement of the Arts, 46

Simpson College, 22, 23, 61
Story of Dr. Carver, The (film), 67
Tuskegee Normal and Industrial Institute, 27, 29, 30, 32, 34, 36, 37, 38, 40, 41, 43, 45, 46, 55, 56, 61, 65, 67, 71
United Daughters of the Confederacy, 56–57

Washington, Booker T., 27, 30, 31, 36, 37, 39, 41, 45, 71

When, What and How To Can and Preserve Fruits and Vegetables in the Home (newsletter), 36

Lois P. Nicholson holds a bachelor of science degree in elementary education and a master's degree in education from the Salisbury State University. She has worked as a school librarian in both an elementary and a middle school in Rock Hall, Maryland. She has written two biographies in the Chelsea House BLACK AMERICANS OF ACHIEVEMENT series: *Oprah Winfrey* and *Michael Jackson*. Additionally, she has written *Cal Ripken, Jr.: Quiet Hero*. Currently she is writing children's biographies on Georgia O'Keeffe, Casey Stengel, Nolan Ryan, Helen Keller, Lucille Ball, and Babe Ruth. Lois Nicholson lives in Baltimore, Maryland.

Picture Credits

AP/Wide World: p. 67; The Bettmann Archive: pp. 14, 21, 30; Courtesy the George Washington Carver Monument: pp. 16, 59; Culver Pictures: p. 6; Department of Agriculture: p. 40; Iowa State University: pp. 2, 26, 47; Library of Congress: pp. 28, 32, 35, 42, 50, 52, 62, 70; Tuskegee Institute: pp. 11, 56.